JEFFANOO

STORIES FROM MY LIFE

JEFFREY ROSE

outskirts
press

Outskirts Press, Inc.
http://www.outskirtspress.com

ISBN: 978-1-9772-2530-6

PRINTED IN THE UNITED STATES OF AMERICA

Table of Contents

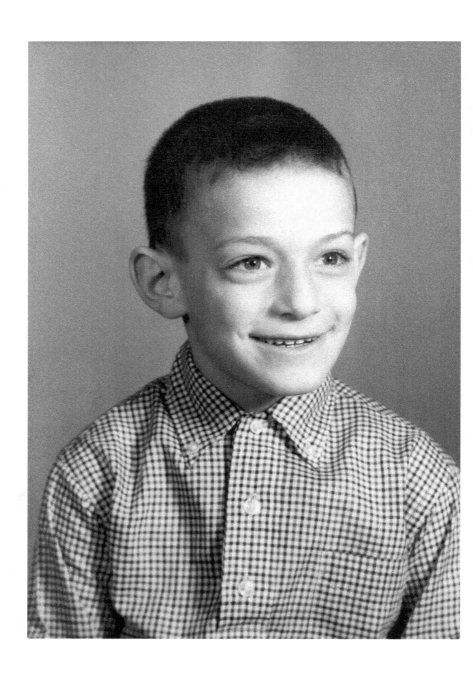

THE EARLY YEARS

I had a wonderful childhood. I remember walking to the swimming pool passing a house where some people had just moved in. It felt good that there would be new friends to meet. People equaled friends.

President of my junior high school seventh grade class. All of the grade schools in the Parkway School District were combined at the junior high level which meant there were eight hundred students in the seventh grade class.

Drinking Dad's Soda

SITTING AT THE kitchen table was a joy! Sharing thoughts feelings, listening and being heard. At peace. We had dinner every night when Dad got home from work about 5:30. It was always a good meal.

I remember sitting next to Dad and drinking his soda. Finished mine and his looked so good. Full of ice and not even touched. I snuck a quick sip. Then another till it was about half gone.

"Jeffrey that's enough", I smiled I was caught. It looked so good one more sip.

He looked at Mom.

"Jeffrey honey that's enough" she said.

Thanks Mom

WE'D GO SHOPPING for school clothes at the end of the summer. Boyd's was a nice clothing store pretty upscale. I found a pair of pants I really liked, but they were forty dollars. The pants were made of gold fleece or some kind of thick felt material. Gold, bellbottom hip huggers. Skin tight. They fit perfect. Perfect. It was a little warm to wear them on the first day of school, but they were my first day of school pants! "Where'd you get those pants?" they'd ask eventually, after they came back from awe.

Oh My Mini Bike!

WASN'T GOING TO have a Bar Mitzvah. At the last minute I changed my mind and decided to have one if the chance still existed. My friends had been going to Hebrew school after regular school for a couple of years, which seemed torturous. It was about a year out from my thirteenth birthday. I got private tutoring in the evening twice a week from Mrs. Weingart.

Dad told me that he would buy anything I wanted for a Bar Mitzvah present, as long as he could afford it. I couldn't believe it. Was he serious? I thought for about five minutes, a mini bike came to mind, but that may be out of the question, too dangerous, too expensive. I waited a minute. Thought about it. Was there anything else I would rather have? He did say anything.

A mini bike.

He said, OK.

Wow!

I asked when I could get it, the Bar Mitzvah wasn't for another year. He said we could go looking the following weekend.

We went to a place where Dad knew the owner. I guess he was a customer of Dad's at his gas station. I don't remember the place that well. A showroom with light brown paneling and several different models of mini bikes, all very nice. I decided on the one I wanted, and we got it, a Fox Campus mini bike. Beautiful. Blue and white with a comfortable white cushion seat and thick tires. What pleasure I got from that thing!

My Dad

I TOLD THIS story to my advisory class today. I think they were tenth graders.

During summer vacation, when I was about thirteen years old and my brother Cliff was about sixteen, I was in our bedroom hanging out with my new friend Charlie, who I really liked. My brother came into the room and got behind me and started choking me. This was fine with me as I greatly enjoyed our playful wrestling throughout the day. However, this time he was rougher than usual. While he was choking me I passed out and fell to the floor. When I hit the floor I banged my head and my whole body stiffened up. Yeah really. This stiffening up propelled my body a few inches forward just under my bed. I hit the bridge of my nose on the metal frame of the bed, which made a little gash. After a few seconds, I came to. My brother Cliff was wide eyed, mouth open. I felt kind of weird, like, "What happened?"

I didn't say anything about the gash on my nose all week. At dinner the following week someone asked me how I got the cut on my nose. I couldn't hold it in any longer, I thought for a moment and decided it had been long enough, it was safe to tell what happened. I asked Mom and Dad to promise they wouldn't do anything to Cliff, if I told them what had happened. My Mom sidestepped this request, and didn't want to commit to the promise. But I refused to go any further with the story without them giving me their promises. They both agreed and I told them what had happened. Within a matter of minutes after hearing what had happened Dad told me to go get Cliff. He was at our subdivision swimming pool. I reminded them that they had promised. But Dad just got more intense, "Go get your brother!" I shut up and went.

On our walk home from the pool Cliff right away asked, "You didn't tell them what happened did you?" I slowly responded, "Yeah, but they promised that they wouldn't do anything to you." He didn't look at me or talk the rest of the way home. When we got there, Dad and Cliff immediately went downstairs. I thought Cliff was going to kill me after this, but to my relief, I never heard another word about it until over fifty years later. He told me that Dad beat him, with his fists.

Straight A's

FOR OUR BIRTHDAYS we decided to celebrate by getting drunk. Not fake drunk or acting drunk, but really drunk. Was it even possible?

We were in Bob's basement with a couple of other friends. Plenty of bourbon snitched from Bob's dad's liquor cabinet along with twenty packets of whiskey sour mix we had purchased. Pour one and a half ounces of bourbon into glass add whiskey sour mix, stir and down the hatch. I did three of these in about ten minutes. Nothing. Three more in about ten more minutes. Maybe a little dizziness. Another three over the next fifteen minutes. I was starting to feel something. One more for good measure. That should do it.

Some girl friends were baby sitting up the street at Biseman's. Why don't we go over there (and show them we're drunk). I fell face first into their house.

"Oh, he's probably faking." some girl said. Then, "Boys you have to leave your gonna wake-up the kids."

We left. I remember somebody hitting me hard in the arm a couple of times and truthfully I barely felt it. He said, "He's really drunk." I was proud. We started walking in the direction of the subdivision swimming pool. That was the last thing I remembered.

I woke up on top of my sister's bed with a different pair of pants on. Who's pants were these and how did I get them on?

Mom poked her head in the room and asked in a cynical tone, "How are you doing?"

"How'd I get these pants on?"

"I have no idea. Marsha and David said they found you past out in a ditch near the swimming pool. She must have changed your pants."

A twinge of fear. Did they see my hairlessness?

"I'm gonna get straight A's Mom." She shouted in the hallway. "Straight A's." Suddenly a picture flashed of Mom helping me into the bedroom and me slurring, "I'm gonna get straight A's."

Grounded for two weeks. I had never been grounded before. This was going to be tough, two weeks. I was surprised when she let me go out that afternoon.

My Trip to England

1969 A YEAR of accomplishment, moon landing, St. Louis Arch, Jerry and Jeff in England. I was fourteen and Jerry sixteen. Jerry lived up the street. His brother David had a charter airline service that flew from Toronto to Heathrow. The cost was one hundred and fifty dollars round trip. He had one seat that wasn't sold and told Jerry he could have it for free. Jerry asked me if I wanted to go with him. We could have the two seats for seventy five dollars apiece.

Would my parents let me go? I had very little travel experience. Jerry was the experienced one. Jerry didn't have the seventy five dollars for his share so I lent it to him.

At dinner that night while we finished eating. I just kind of slid the question in the middle of conversation. "If I had the money would it be OK if I went to England?" They kind of nodded yes, that it would be OK and we moved on to another conversation.

Four days later at dinner I said, "Well I'm going to England." They both looked at me. What?

"I'm going to England. You said I could and I've ordered my passport."

"Oh no you're not! What do you mean we said it was OK", Mom asked?

"Don't you remember? A couple of days ago at dinner I asked you if I had the money could I go to England and you said yes."

"Oh no you're not buster. How do you plan on going to England?"

"Jerry's brother David has a charter service to England and he has an empty seat. He told Jerry that he could have it for free. So all we have to do is pay seventy five dollars apiece. I've got the money. I told him you said yes and I've already ordered my passport specially from Chicago."

"I don't think you can go, but your father and I will discuss it."

I was all set to go ready to walk out of the house and over to Jerry's. When Mom came close, looked at me and said "Promise me you won't do anything illegal and no marijuana."

I thought for a moment and said "Don't worry we won't do anything wrong and we'll be careful."

"Promise me or you're not going."

I promised.

The charter was for six weeks and left from Toronto. We hitch hiked from St. Louis to Toronto. We had three bags between us. One was a long duffle that held our tent. It was pretty heavy. I was worried that I was going to end up carrying it most of the time. Since we were hitching we didn't know how long it would take us to get there. We couldn't risk getting there late and losing our seats. We built in for this by adding an extra four days for travel. We were lucky and quickly got rides all the way there. We arrived at the Toronto airport three days early. Three days.

This was Toronto's second airport. Not very big. It was built in the shape of a circle. One of the fun things we did, until the authorities made us quit, was push each other around the circle in wheel chairs. We met two other guys at the airport and played poker. We had our money, mostly change, next to us on the floor while we played. The police said it was illegal to gamble there and made us quit. Chased by the Royal Canadian Police. Everyone was happy when the time finally came and we flew in a prop jet an eighteen hour flight to Heathrow.

Kind of neat Heathrow airport England. We walked out to the road and hitch hiked toward the docks at Tilbury. We decided to go to Sweden by ship. I thought there would be naked women in the streets in Sweden. On rides to the docks Jerry sat in the front seat and I sat in the back. I couldn't understand a word of what the drivers were saying it was like a different language. We hitched most of the first day with me carrying the heavy duffle most of the time. Somehow we couldn't find our way to the shipping docks. First we were told to take the A ten highway which we couldn't locate. Turned out it wasn't the A ten it was the I ten. Then we couldn't find The Woods Inn. It wasn't the Woods Inn it was the Worlds Inn. It was dusk we were exhausted. Somewhere near London at a lovely spot overlooking the Thames there was a grassy area close to the road. We pitched our tent.

How did I get into this? Why did they let me go? What were we going to do for five more weeks? I slept for fifteen hours that night.

Jerry was into music and he knew about a rock festival in the town of Plumpton. Plumpton was near the southern coast of England. We found a place that rented motor scooters and rented a grey Vespa along with two helmets. The cost was fifty or sixty dollars for a week. Jerry had a drivers license. He did a great job of driving us but one time we were making a turn around a corner and he somehow lost control. We started going down our helmets bowled across the street hitting the curb before we hit the ground. Fortunately we were OK and the scooter only a scratch.

At the festival we found a spot and put up the tent. The night before the festival there was a large tent with music and a few colored lights streaming along the tent walls. Some people talked some swayed to the music arms waving. I tried to do this but felt like I didn't fit in, too stiff. Too conscious?

Jerry wanted to buy some marijuana but I was hesitant. I had promised. Jerry purchased some hashish from someone in the big tent and we went back to our tent to try it out. It was the real thing. We heard some good music, Yes and Cat Stevens. The last night when we went back to our tent my sleeping bag was missing. I froze that night.

In the morning Jerry went to the police station to see if my bag was in lost and found. There were other sleeping bags there, but not mine. We didn't want to spend the money but I had to have a sleeping bag. Jerry suggested I claim one of the bags at the station, how would they know the difference? Jerry would swing by later to pick me up. I surveyed the sleeping bags on the shelf behind the counter and picked one that resembled mine.

"Are you sure that is your sleeping bag" the policeman behind the counter asked?

"Yes, that's it."

He came around from behind the counter sat beside me and asked questions about the bag.

"When did you notice it was missing? How much did you pay for it?"

He went on for a half hour writing everything down. When he was done he informed me that they caught the thief who stole the bag and that I would have to press charges. I told him that I didn't want to press charges. He said I had to. All that I had to do was say it was my sleeping bag. Well I couldn't do it. Not if it wasn't my bag.

"It's not mine."

"What?"

"It's not really my sleeping bag. I can't press charges if it's not really mine."

His demeanor changed drastically. He said wait right here and walked away.

He came back and said "Your under arrest."

I remembered that Jerry was coming to get me that he had the hash in his shirt pocket. I thought of the promise to Mom and started sobbing and sobbing.

They put me in the back of a police car and drove off to the jail. Jerry yelled out to me that he would meet us at the jail. I was glad to see him, but worried about what he was carrying. I had a sense that they weren't really going to arrest me, that they were just trying to scare me. They took me into the jail and fingerprinted me, took my belt and cap, searched around the rim. Still felt fairly certain that they were just trying to scare me. They put me behind bars where there was a bench to sit on. There was another young person there.

"What did I do" he asked?

"Claimed a sleeping bag that wasn't mine."

They took the other guy out and I sat there for a short time before they came and got me. They were smiling. They decided not to arrest me. I was relieved but acted even more thankful and relieved to make sure they were satisfied. We had to go to the American Embassy within forty eight hours to inform them what happened or get deported.

The crime that I was charged with had a long name three sentences long. Jerry wanted to purposely get deported. That way we would get a free ride back and sell our tickets. We would never be allowed back into the country again. No thanks! Let's get this done.

In London we stayed at a youth hostel and explored the city. A.E. Richard's Fish and Chips. Delish! Wrapped in paper with fried potatoes, catsup, vinegar and pickled onions.

Caught strep and had to go to the doctor. No health insurance. I was quickly seen by a doctor and given a prescription of penicillin all for a couple of dollars. We took a hovercraft across the channel to France. Tried to make it to Paris, but ended up just north in Lille. We couldn't explain to the bus driver or concerned passengers where we wanted to go. We pitched our tent in what turned out to be a cemetery in a dangerous part of town. We hustled back to England the next day.

I had wealthy relatives in London, Annie and Ike. They were in the clothing business. We finally contacted them on our last day. Their chofur picked us up in a Citroen and drove us to the daughter's home. The table for lunch had lots of forks, knives and spoons. We talked about our trip and family news. They were glad we got to meet, but were surprised our parents allowed us to go at such young ages. He showed us pictures of himself with the Queen touring his clothing plant. Jerry talked me into hitting them up for money. He frowned but gave me the ten pounds I asked for.

We spent two days at Heathrow airport. All night long bing bing bing, British United Airways, bing bing bing, Trans World Airlines ... Our flight back to Toronto was much faster and on a regular jet. We hitched a long ride almost all the way home.

The kitchen was dark and quiet. Wanted to hear all about it tomorrow or when I was ready. She could get some sleep.

HIGH SCHOOL

Thirty Hours on a Bus

THIRTY HOURS ON a bus. Not too bad. We sat in the very back seats. Alex had thirty hours of music on his cassettes we could just listen to music for the thirty hours. How long is a school day? Six hours. This was five of those!

What a trip. There was the guy who was going to Rome. Rome, Georgia. The guy who had the bottle of vodka which was passed around until the bus was spinning. The women who I sat next to. I'd say she was about early twenties. Black hair. It took a little courage to make the first kiss. Making out on the bus. She was a smoker. "How old are you fifteen?" Then she got off at the next stop.

After our Spring Break in Nassau we hitched back home. To avoid the tortuous ride and save money.

Smith Pants

THEY WERE PURCHASED at an army salvage store. Straight leg blue jean pants. Not regular blue jeans. Light weight, real baggy. They were a good fit no need for a belt and I don't remember them having any belt loops. There was a white patch on the back near the top that had the name Smith printed. Didn't think much of it. They were comfortable and I wore them to school. Well they became kind of a thing, the Smith pants. Hey, you don't question these things. One afternoon my friend Alex and I were sitting at my kitchen table. Just sitting there when Mom comes up from downstairs. She had been doing laundry. She had the pants in her hand.

I think these pants have a little rip", she said.

"Oops it's a big rip", and she tore them in half as she laughed.

Alex said in terror, "No, not the Smith pants!"

My heart sank. We looked at each other eyebrows raised. It was a fate complete.

Wrote this poem for an English class the night before our final project was due. We had all semester to work on it. I copied a few other published poems on a piece of paper and asked Bill Simpson, in the previous class to make drawings next to each poem. He agreed and the drawings were great!

Purpose

Why go to school ?

I know how to speak

I'd rather just be a freak.

Why go to school ?

I know how to add

I'd rather just sit around the pad.

Is having a profession the ultimate goal?

I think I would rather crawl in a hole.

Suzy

WE MET AT a weekend sensitivity training group. Our first date is kind of a blur, idyllic, comfortable. I was nervous but it went smoothly. We went to Fleur de lis restaurant in Kirkwood. I walked her to the door kissed her goodbye.

She was the eldest of four and she was bossy to them, but she was never that way to me. The first time she ever told me to do something we were driving in my car after school with some of her friends. We drove around a figure eight off ramp which made us lean as we went around. As a joke I went around again. Everyone giggled but as we finished the second loop Suzy said, "Don't do it again." It kind of jerked my whole being. In retrospect it was probably one of her friends who told her to tell me this.

After about two months of seeing each other every weekend we had sex. It was at my sister's one bedroom apartment. It was romantic and beautiful naturally just like all of our time together. We used a rubber for protection. She told her mother and she got her on the Pill. It took two weeks before we were able to make love carefree. So simple and easy why didn't everyone use birth control pills?

She broke up with me her senior year when I went away to Southwest Missouri State University. Crushed. Addicted to sex.

Creve Coeur

"Good night. I love you."

"Good night. Take care."

No, there must be a mistake!

"Good night. I love you."

"Take care."

Click.

King Dink

WENT OUT FOR the tennis team to impress Suzy. Southwest Missouri State had a pretty good team, recruited throughout the state. I didn't even play in high school! Here's the way I thought and played: make sure it doesn't go in net, hit it high as you want but not past baseline, chase ball down, repeat.

That's what I did. It wasn't pretty. Hit it to me and *boomph* up she goes back to ya. *Wheee* up she goes until you miss. Sometimes the opponent would think, "I can do that" and start airing it back to me the same way. We had long points but I won most of them and my opponent went back to his own style and started throwing his racquet. There were six singles and three doubles on the starting lineup with number one being our top player. I played at number six to number four. Coach Richard Fronabarger was a tennis fanatic from birth. He had challenge matches for my position every day. I never lost.

AFTER COLLEGE

Majored in Biology and Psychology. But just slid by, C average. Five years to graduate at least it was done. Couldn't find a job in either field. I graduated in May, 1977 and Dad died four months later. A poker friend's father owned Hacienda restaurant. Got a job there as a waiter. The place was busy and I made pretty good money while living at home. I met a waitress there. She was married with two small children. I fixed up my new red Chevy van and headed out to California. Escaped from living at home cramping my mother's style and from a relationship with a married women.

The Van

I WENT TO the race track with a group of friends specifically to bet on one horse, Van's Hope. On the way to the track we were play acting, "And they're off. They're half way round the first turn and its Van's Hope against the rail in the middle of the pack. It's Van's Hope moving up to third. And it's Van's Hope pulling ahead and it's Van's Hope by a neck." He was a sixty to one shot facing Sarnoff the fastest horse at the track. I bet $25 on the Hope, something like $10 to win, $10 to place and $5 to show. The way we acted people must have thought we won a million bucks! Particularly Harold. He was a big guy. He raised his hands over his head and his scream shook the earth.

I used the money to make a down payment on a new red Chevy van. A few months later I fixed it up with paneling, a bed and a dresser and headed out to California to seek my fortune. On the way I stopped in Las Vegas.

There are not many things more thrilling than the excitement of a poker game. Poker was a part of our lives then. On the bus on the way home from school, we decided whose home the game would be at. I stopped in Las Vegas to see what I could do. One thing was certain, I had logged in time at the table. I parked the van in the overnight campers site. I was there for six weeks barely holding my own. My last day there was the big game.

I went to the MGM Grand and sat at the five and ten table (all the tables were seven card stud in 1979). There was a tall bald man sitting at the end of the table to my right and on the other end of the table was a women that he knew and they were joking with each other. The first two hours, I was slowly losing. I was down to two or three hundred dollars when the big hand came. I was dealt a medium pair down, which I bet. On the fifth card I was dealt a pair up and bet the ten dollar limit. The bald guy on the end raised me and I raised him and he raised back. Everyone else folded. After the sixth card all I had was a low two pair. The bald man bet and I raised and he just called. On the seventh card I drew a full house. My heart was smiling. He bet, I raised, he raised and I raised. Almost immediately after we showed our hands he stood up and started shouting. He was tall. He walked around to the end of the table near the women he knew, and he was talking loud! He yelled something like, "He pulled it on the last card!"

I felt really good. I thought I was a stud. But somewhere inside I was scared by this guy. At first he said he was going to get a new dealer, but instead just had him open a new deck. I was back all the money I had lost plus a few hundred. We continued play and for the next two or three hours I didn't win a hand. When I finally won a small hand everyone was glad for me. I lost all my money and had to quit.

From Las Vegas I travelled to California. I stopped in Sacramento where I had a pick up racquetball game with a guy I met at a sports club. I told him my situation, that I had fixed up this van and was travelling to seek my fortune. He told me that he worked for a photographic plate company in

San Diego where everybody played racquetball and had a biology background. He was sure they would hire me. The next day I headed to San Diego.

The trip to San Diego had shimmering colors like a Cezanne painting. I located the photographic plate company, parked the van on a Safeway parking lot, and set up an interview. I interviewed for the position for three weeks. The final interview was with Takahashi the supervisor. He said there was a lot of material to learn and asked me if I was willing to put in the time and effort to learn it? I paused and thought about it, hemmed and hawed a little then said something like, "I'll work pretty hard, but I'm not going to devote my whole life to it."

It wasn't long before I ran out of money. I was used to being on college campuses at the athletic facilities and hung around the nearby University of San Diego. I placed an ad for my van in the newspaper and used the phone number of the pay phone just outside of the racquetball courts for my contact number. I had seventy five cents left over. Enough to buy a newspaper to see the ad, call Reggie in Houston to tell her I was coming and to call home if I was flat broke.

I got to the phones early and sat down on the grass. I felt kind of stupid sitting there. The phone rang. Wrong number. I checked to make sure the ad was in the paper with the right phone number. When the phone finally rang again, it was about the van. The caller wanted to come by and take a look at it. He made me an offer of $3,900. I was asking $4,200. I countered back at $4,100 and he said $4,000 was his final offer. I stuck at $4,100 and he agreed.

We went to his bank to get a cashier's check and on the way I asked if he would take me to the airport? He realized that I had few belongings and couldn't believe I held firm at the $4,100 price.

Longshoreman

WHEN I MOVED to Houston I lived with my girlfriend Reggie for about a month then we broke up. I moved to an apartment in the Montrose area. The apartment was pretty stark. Second story of a two story building, it had two rooms of equal size with hardwood floors. One wooden chair. Windows across the whole front of the apartment, with no covering at all, just windows.

I didn't have a job and the money from the sale of the van was running out. I wasn't too concerned, I'd find a job doing something. I didn't have a car. There was a bus stop about two blocks from the apartment. It was 1980 Houston and the town was booming, buses ran irregularly.

This is the story that my brother loves. I even told it at his wedding. I tried working as a longshoreman. I caught the bus at 5:30am, made two transfers to arrive at the Port of Houston at 6:30am. This was when extra workers were hired. *Casual men* gathered in a room with a raised wooden platform in the front. The walking boss came out on the platform, looked over the group and picked as many workers as needed for the day. I had a hard hat with ROSE printed on the front. The walking boss called your name and the type of job he had for you, "Jones, rice" or "Sanchez, hides". The job paid one hundred dollars a day. I got picked about once every four or five times that I tried.

I heard there were some jobs you didn't want to do, like loading steel poles since they were unstable and fell on people. One morning the walking boss came out, surveyed the room, looked at me and said, "Rose, hook-on". I was excited to be picked, but still asked, "What's hook-on?" He looked at me briefly then said, "Ramirez, hook-on". The room cleared out and the hired people went to their jobs. Later I found out what hook-on meant, every fifteen minutes or so a line swung from a crane to you on the dock and you attached the hook to the load.

I was two weeks late for rent and started feeling the pinch. I went downtown into office buildings, looked at the marquises for interesting jobs and knocked on doors. At one building I went to a newspaper office, and told the receptionist I was looking for a job.

"You must be looking for the reporter position", she said.

Somewhat surprised, I shook my head in agreement. I interviewed for the position, but didn't get the job. In another office building I saw on the marquise Allseas Shipping Company. There were several doors which had that name on them, but the offices were all empty. As I was leaving a man on the elevator asked me what I was looking for. I told him Allseas Shipping. He said that was his company. Jerry Lane was a handsome, balding man. I told him that I was looking for a job. He was heading down to the docks and asked if I wanted to go with him. He was in a hurry but we could talk on the way.

We drove to a sporting goods store and he literally ran to the back of the store where the gun section was. He quickly looked over the guns in the case and selected a pistol. He had a trucking business across the street from the sporting goods store, which they called to verify his identity. He paid them four hundred dollars for a pistol and we ran out of the store with me running behind him thinking, what is going on?

Back in the car he asked me if I had a driver's license. I hadn't driven since I sold my van two months ago. He started giving me directions on how to get to the Port. We stopped at a nearby parking lot where there was a new Honda. I hopped into the car and followed behind him speeding and weaving down the highway to the Port. At the Port we drove behind loading platforms with mini trucks going in and out. He was flying. We drove out onto the dock and he ran onto a ship. Jerry was relieved that he got to the ship before it took off for Ecuador. Driving back to his office he told me that the captain of the ship had trouble with his crew and needed a gun.

After this special interview, I felt like I had earned my stripes and had a good shot at getting a job. He told me to come back the next day and we could talk further about it. I came back the next day but he was too busy to talk. I came back again and he hired me as a salesman selling space on an Ecuadorian flag ship the Pinchecha.

I didn't know what I was supposed to do. There were three of us in this big office space, Jerry, a secretary and me. The reason for all this empty space was that Allseas Shipping had lost their big account, Rollo Pacific. I felt competition from the secretary. She was young and single with a small child and no education. What was I doing there that she couldn't do? I eventually earned her respect.

I had my own office and spent the first week trying to figure out what a salesman for a shipping company did. I read everything in the office. Jerry was always busy and I was a little afraid of him. What I learned was that we sold space on the Pinchecha and loaded it with freight going from Houston to Ecuador.

I didn't like the uncomfortable feeling that I had with Jerry, and I had a fear that I wasn't going to be paid. After two months I quit. The day that I quit happened to be the day that the owner of the Pinchecha came to the office to meet with us. In the morning Jerry was excited about the owner coming then he was really disappointed when I told him I was quitting. When I had trouble finding another job and the rent was overdue, I realized quitting had been a little hasty.

Once again I walked around downtown looking for work. When I was getting ready to catch the bus home a silver and gold animal sculpture with elephants on the wall caught my attention. It led to the door of Harry's Kenya restaurant. Harry's Kenya was a fancy new downtown restaurant. I wondered in. The manager, Merle, his assistant, Eddy and Eddy's wife Yolaine were fun loving people and I was kind of a free spirit that they were attracted to. They hired me as a waiter.

I worked there for two years. An eternity. I worked lunches ten to two Monday to Friday. It was a forty dollars a day lunch. I could live on that. What the hell enjoy your time here.

The place was jammed every day. This was downtown boomtown Houston. We had three person teams; captain, waiter, bus person. This was the best system for service. The captain took the order and gave it to the waiter, the waiter picked up the food from the kitchen and served it, the bus person cleared and reset the table. Any more people than that and communication broke down.

I had a busboy named Louis. He didn't speak much English at first. A good worker and reliable. He was also gentle. We worked together for a while and made a good two thirds of a team. Over time we had several waiters. After the rush one day Louis kept saying a word to me and smiling. I didn't understand. Finally I understood. He was saying the name of our waiter who was a nice guy but a *zapatero* (shoe maker).

I gave good service and was proud of the work I did, but wasn't proud of my station in life. Women were less proud.

Waiting in the Food Pickup Line at Harry's Kenya

WE WERE STANDING in line waiting to pickup our food orders. Dark tan, oval food trays lined up on the metal rail facing the cooks. Mike was right next to me in line.

"I kill somebody today *chrrumph*!", he uttered and gazed ahead.

This was a fancy lunch in boomtown Houston. A battle every lunch. I'd been through the drill for over a year. There wasn't any rookie of only two days who was gonna bother me.

"I kill somebody today *chrrumph*!"

He turned his glaze at me. I moved to the end of the line.

The Port

I REMEMBER THE first day. Standing there looking into the dining room with the red flocked wall paper. I had come from very exclusive restaurants. Here I was at The Port St. Louis. Jeez, it was tacky. However, it turned out to be a great place with professional waiters. We were busy every night at The Port. What made us that busy at an expensive restaurant with average not fancy food? It was sexy and it was service. I knew good service. I had worked at La Reserve, Harry's Kenya, and The Remington in Houston Texas. I made sure we gave good service. I made sure that things were done a certain way and they knew that Wade would make sure.

Charles

He was the number one waiter. His was the best station in the house. He told me about an attractive women who used to sit at the end of the bar on Friday nights where she could see his station. One night he asked her why she sat there. She said she just liked to watch him work. I got to work with him once on New Year's Eve. We made two hundred dollars each in tips that night. I tried my best to be up to his level.

Leroy

On a busy Saturday night we were just running no time to think. Leroy asked me for a bottle of wine. I was in the wine cellar with the bottle in hand when Leroy came in like a tornado, "Where's the wine", he hissed? I felt like hitting him with it. I said, "I love you Leroy". He looked at me calmly took the bottle and left.

One evening when we were setting up for dinner there was a call on the pay phone. It was Leroy he asked to speak to Wade. Wade told me that Leroy wouldn't be coming in that night. What happened? Wade wouldn't just let something go like that very easily. I found out later that Leroy was drunk.

One night it was late and we still had a reservation for ten coming in. I asked who would stay to take the party and Leroy volunteered. When they arrived the restaurant was empty. I was tired. Leroy took over. He asked one lady if he could feed her and she let him.

Duff

He was so smooth and soft. He had a few parties that just loved him. They were his parties.

Arthur

He was their kitchen man. He was big and tough. He could carry sixteen dinners.

Larry

He was white. He also had his special parties. He didn't jump for anybody. I remember watching him clear a table, "See how he did that?" pointing to the person seated next to him who had neatly stacked his plate and silverware.

At about five thirty every evening the waiters would start getting antsy.

"There's no business tonight, can I take off? Let some people go. Nobody's going to make any money."

Well this was my decision. We were a popular place in an upscale business area. We generally had good walk in business. On this particular night the waiters were really on me,

"Let some people go nobody's going to make any money."

Finally I relented and let a few waiters go home. Well we got busy. Everybody worked their tails off customers were happy. We gave great service just like always.

The next night before we opened, Wade gathered all the waiters together and gave us hell.

"We did a hundred and twenty people and we only had six waiters! There couldn't have been good service."

"But we did Wade", I tried to assure him.

"There's no way!"

Arthur said, "That's his fault Wade. Not ours."

The night before it was Arthur who complained the loudest about letting people off.

Sylvia and the Cold Call

WE WERE IN the real estate business. One evening me and Sylvia (my Aunt Zel) were the only ones in the office. We were sitting pretty near each other near the back of the room. This was a tense time making cold calls to list property for sale.

Sylvia had someone on the line and was talking. Then I heard her get a little louder and she said,

"Oh, I'm so glad you're not dead!"

I turned around to look at her with my mouth open. She had taken names from the obituaries and was making calls to see if the relatives wanted to sell their property. Well the person she was speaking to said it was him and he wasn't dead.

Many years later she pointed out the property she had called about that evening. A valuable commercial piece that had since been developed. Worth the risk of embarrassment.

Cytology

WASN'T MAKING IT in real estate. Saw an ad in the newspaper for a cytotechnologist. I knew that *cyto* meant cell in Latin, had liked cell biology in college. Applied for the job but needed certification. To get certification you went to school for a year then took an exam. There were twenty schools in the country. Most of them only had three or four students. The State Laboratory of Hygiene at the University of Wisconsin, Madison, had twelve students. Their program was full but I was accepted as an alternate. At the beginning of August,1990 they called. A student had changed her mind they had an opening! I didn't know what a cytotechnologist did. School started in two weeks.

Loaded up my green Galaxy 500 and drove to Madison. Went to a nice residential neighborhood near campus and knocked on the door of one of the homes. They didn't rent to students but the family across the street did. It was an impressive three story brick home at the top of a hill. I took a deep breath and knocked on the door. An attractive women in her late forties answered. She invited me into her home. There was an immediate connection. They had a room available on the third floor with a female medical student living there, we would share a bathroom and kitchen.

The building was old but well maintained. Small kitchen with a sloping, freshly painted grey cement floor. I moved my stuff into a room on the third floor. There wasn't a bed. That night when Dr. Barash came home we hoisted a mattress and box spring up to the third floor using a pulley, an impressive powerful force. The Barashs were a conservative Jewish family with three sons. Two teenage sons lived at home, the eldest was away at medical school. Nice family, gorgeous place to stay, reasonable rate, walk to school. Not bad!

The State Laboratory of Hygiene had its own cytology lab with ten cytotechnologists. Lynn Sterude was our teacher and John Shalkham was her assistant. Two veteran cytotechs with a balance of hard work and silliness. Class was eight hours a day, we were a competitive group in a challenging program. We welcomed a release!

Pathologists taught the human biology sections, we rotated through prep lab, genetics lab and gynecology. To complete the program a term paper was required. Mine was titled, *Mechanisms of Human Papillomavirus Oncogenisis in the Uterine Cervix*. Human papillomavirus (HPV) infection, particularly with strains 16 and 18, were known to be directly involved in the transformation process. Several years later I published an article in the California Association of Cytotechnology Newsletter with the same title.

There was a twenty percent vacancy rate for cytotechs! After completing school and passing the test I immediately received calls from laboratories. One call was from Pathology Services in Berkeley, California. They had recently lost two cytotechs and had a long backlog of Pap smears to be screened. They flew me out to Berkeley and put me up in The Claremont Hotel.

Jane Zaloudek and Dr. Charles Zaloudek, were part

owners of Pathology Services, Jane was CEO and Dr. Zaloudek was a pathologist. They took me out to lunch at Chez Panisse. Jane offered me the wine list, Dr. Zaloudek reached to take it from her but she insisted I make the selection. Kenwood, sauvignon blanc was a safe choice.

After five years you qualify to sit for the Specialist in Cytotechnology exam. Studied for six months and took the exam. My strategy was to go through and answer all the questions I knew then go back and do the rest. This helped build confidence. The first five questions didn't know any of them, the next five same thing, five more not even one. How could this be? A few weeks later got the results. Pass. My fifty percent score was enough.

My Mom

IT WAS OUR annual holiday party. We walked from the car up to Dr. Salyer's home in a nice area of Berkeley. Mom was on a mission. She didn't wait for me. She was happy and walked on ahead. I didn't see her for the rest of the evening. The next day and for the rest of the years I worked there people who I didn't even know would ask,

"How's your Mom"?

She was on a mission; implacable, confident, smiling and proud when she looked at me.

Back to St. Louis

PATHOLOGY SERVICES WAS a great place to work, quality lab, didn't push you for numbers, good pay with profit sharing. But the job was hard and time crept by. After seven and a half years I made a change. Moved back to St. Louis and moved in with my mother. Relaxed for a few months, worked out at the Jewish Community Center, and joined Traditional Congregation.

After snarling traffic for ten years, work on Olive Street Boulevard in Chesterfield was finally completed, two clogged lanes were expanded to four fluid lanes. Was this my opportunity? Got the plats for the properties abutting this two mile stretch. Talked with some of the owners but it didn't click. A year and a half went by, still no work. I wasn't in a hurry, booked a hiking trip across Israel through a travel agent at synagogue. Mom was incensed! She didn't want me going on a trip without first having a job. At the last minute cancelled the trip. There were openings for cytotechnologists at Quest Diagnostics close to home. Back in cytology.

The Toast

WE HADN'T BEEN seeing each other that long when we went out to dinner with her parents. Her two young children weren't with us. I felt compelled to make a toast like I owed them something. I raised my wine glass and said,

"I'd like to make a toast to you and your beautiful daughter. She is so wonderful to be with. Thank you for bringing her into the world."

It wasn't exactly flowing out of me. An uncomfortable silence. They just looked at me. What was I talking about? Was it true what I said? Maybe that was how I hoped it would be.

No Proposal

WE MET IN synagogue. She was there for evening minion for her deceased husband's yartzeit (anniversary of his death). I was there saying evening prayers. I knew her name, Lori, because a high school acquaintance told me if he was single she was who he would go after. When I heard her name at synagogue my antenna went up. After talking with her a few times we went out on a date.

We went to a vodka bar and she got pretty loaded. When we danced she hung on me with her arms around my neck like dead weight. What was this? Sexy? We moved slowly on the dance floor and didn't sit down in between songs. We were out of beat with the music, too slow.

I was forty years old still searching for myself and for a relationship to take the place of Suzy from high school. When we first met I told her that I would know immediately whether or not she was right for me. We were together twelve years.

One night after about five years of being together, I planned to ask her to marry me. It was just after Shabbat, we had finished singing havdalah (the prayers for the separation of the Sabbath day from the work week). Lori wanted to go out as we had planned, but I wanted to stay home. She wouldn't relent she wanted to go out. I wouldn't give in either because I was going to pop the question. She wanted desperately to get married. She had two children one with Asperger's syndrome.

We couldn't resolve it. She wanted to go out I wanted to stay home. Lori had a tantrum. She was lying on her bed face down totally unresponsive. At first I was worried that she was dying or dead. This went on for several hours. I stopped thinking about asking her to marry and started thinking how to get out.

Back to School

I WAS LAID off from Quest Diagnostics after reading Pap smears there for eight years. I felt bad but didn't know why. Was that how I was supposed to feel?

My brain said, "This is great! My job is too hard. I've been wanting out since I started cytotechnology school eighteen years ago."

But the feeling of dread was real. I chose to become a high school biology teacher. I had an undergraduate degree in biology along with cytology training and had loved high school!

Fifty four years old. If I worked as hard at school as I worked reading Pap smears I couldn't miss. For three years I gave it all I had, never missed a class, always early, homework done. Had been a poor student, this was a chance.

I remember studying for the Physics II final. The teacher gave us the final exams from previous years to study. I could answer all of the questions which took a big effort! Studied all week and late into the morning the night of the final. After the exam I sat on a bench and watched the sun come up over a hill. I was drained but hopeful. I knew I did well. The physics courses were unknowns. If I passed them there wasn't anything standing in my way of becoming a teacher.

After many interviews and several years of substitute teaching, I was finally hired as a full time teacher. Vashon High School had a bad reputation. I thought about the biblical story of the spies. If the Israelites had gone into the promised land as God had directed they could have avoided forty years of wandering in the desert. This was my path into the promised land.

Three weeks of trying my hardest sending one student after another to the office only to have them return and continue disrupting. Tried to quit but they wouldn't allow it. I had signed a year's contract. The following week I went to the principal again. He could tell I was losing it and let me quit. Thank God! Substitute teacher five years. I wanted someone to talk to after my eventful days. To hear my joy and stamp it into the world. Whatever stamp there was only remained in them.

Gravity

I CAN'T BELIEVE I didn't know that everything has gravity. Everything has gravity. It's not a theory. We know it. It's measurable and has been measurable since 1798. When I was subbing we often discussed the formula for measuring gravity:

$$\text{Gravity} = (6.67 \times 10^{-11}) \frac{\text{Mass 1} \times \text{Mass 2}}{\text{Distance}^2}$$

This is a large number. It's good to get students used to playing with big numbers. It's not that difficult of an equation. It's important!

What the hell is gravity? I was an assistant special education teacher at Hake Middle School in St. Louis and somehow got to teach a few minutes at the end of a history class. I told them that gravity was the weakest force in the Universe. One student asked what was the strongest force? I told him that I didn't know. The bell rang and I gave him the assignment to find out what was the strongest force and report it to the class.

The next day I totally forgot about this assignment. Between classes a student nudged me in the hall and said,

"I found out what the strongest force is."

"What?"

"I found out what the strongest force is."

"What is it?"

"The force of nuclear energy", he said proudly!

I was proud too.

Teaching Fifth Graders About Cancer

WHEN I WAS a substitute teacher I always told my classes a little bit about myself. As long as I fulfilled the regular teacher's lesson plans I could teach however and whatever I wanted. The daily lesson plans were already prepared when I arrived. There was vast potential all around!

I worked as a cytotechnologist for sixteen years. Cytotechnologists screen Pap smears. I knew about cells and I knew what cancer looked like under a microscope. They were too young to discuss Pap smears so I told them that I looked at cells for cancer. I showed them on the board what cells looked like and what cancerous changes looked like. I showed them how easy it was to tell between a normal cell and a cancer cell, the latter being much bigger and darker.

When there was a cut in the skin, cells grew faster to repair the cut or in response to an infection there was usually an inflammatory response. Both of these were normal reparative/ inflammatory changes. Deciding between a normal reactive change and cancer was the humbling challenge.

Philosophy of Teaching

by Jeffrey Alan Rose

FOR STUDENTS TO achieve their best, they need clearly defined objectives, along with assessments aligned to measure how well they have learned these objectives. Routines and procedures aid in classroom management, and keep classes flowing smoothly. These routines and procedures need to be taught heavily during the first two weeks of class, along with class rules, and a discipline plan.[1]

I believe in Best Practice methods, and a student centered approach to teaching.[2,3] Students need to be free to express their individuality when learning material. Therefore, I strive to provide choices for students, to learn about what interests them most. Reading and writing are basic to education, and lifelong learning. It is important to provide class time to practice their reading and writing skills.

Modeling and small group activities are important parts of teaching. I like to demonstrate modeling through think aloud activities. Sometimes while reading aloud or writing on the board I tell students what is going through my head at the moment. Using small and medium size group activities allows students to interact with each other, and get feedback from their peers.

I believe in the value of community, and in collaborative teaching. There are resources in the community that should be utilized.[4] Overall, students need to be actively engaged in learning processes; in a caring, positive environment, where all students are expected to succeed.

A Funny Time

WE WERE SITTING in the eye doctor's office, waiting for the doctor. It was Mom's first time to see him. I came prepared with a New Yorker magazine. I was reading about the smartest person in the world competition. There were several individuals touted for this honor. One of these geniuses, spoke nine languages, which kind of floored me. I told Mom about this, and read aloud the list of nine languages.

"I just wish I could remember the doctor's name" she said.

Mom's 90th

ON HER 88TH I didn't have the money but asked her if she wanted to have a birthday celebration and invite the family.

She said, "Let's wait until I'm 90."

I doubted she would live till then.

She was in a nursing home where she'd been for about seven years. Pretty nice place and they had a decent number of Medicaid beds. My mother on Medicaid? Oh yeah! Thank you God. The previous month she had been in rehab, which is in a special section of the home. When she was in that section it was paid for by Medicare, but we still received the monthly Medicaid payment (or something like that). Anyway we had an extra twelve hundred bucks. To be on Medicaid you have to have less than a thousand dollars to your name. We had to spend this extra money.

Delmar Gardens did a great job; they knew how to throw good parties. Also, Kohn's Catering did a great job. Champagne, eggs, bagel and lox. The whole family showed. She made it alright!

A Comment On Money

AT MY FORTY fifth high school reunion I had a brief conversation with Rick and Steve's wife. In high school Rick ran with a tough crowd. Surprisingly Rick was financially successful. Steve's wife had published a cook book.

Rick said, "Your health is everything."

Steve's wife agreed.

I said, "No it's not you've got to have money. To live in this country you have to have money."

The conversation ended and they walked away.

20th High School Reunion

I LOVED HIGH school. Loved it. Maybe because I didn't do any schoolwork, but mostly because I was in love with people and life. Friends. Freedom to express myself. Popular. For some reason I decided to graduate a semester early from this idyllic situation. Not for some reason but because of this: I was home skipping school with Suzy. My next door neighbor came over the house. This was unusual. She was pretty cute, a year older than me and two years older than Suzy.

The neighbor said, "Graduate early if at all possible. That's what I did and I'm so glad!"

My twentieth reunion was a trip. Didn't go to the tenth. Embarrassed about being a waiter in Houston, Texas. At my twentieth, I was living in Walnut Creek, California and was doing something called cytotechnology. I read Pap smears. The reunion was a big deal to me. I was very popular way back then and happy. I wanted to relive those days. Love people like I used to and be loved.

I had a nice blue suit and wanted a great tie to go with it. San Francisco was the place to find one. I started off at one end of Union Square and went all the way around the square looking at ties but with no success. I left for St. Louis without a tie. By Saturday still nothing. This was getting serious. I asked Mom to go with me. We went to about a dozen stores and somewhere in there found a great tie. Some people at the reunion heard about my expedition and said, "Nice tie." Maybe I'll wear it to the fiftieth.

An Influence in My Life

MY PARENTS GAVE me a solid foundation. I felt their uncon-ditional love, and I loved them. Mom was a friend who I could talk to about anything. When I was four years old my brother Cliff told me how babies were made. I said, no way. He said it was right. I said I was going to ask Mom, as I thought this would make him back down. He said go ahead. She thought for a minute, looked at me and said, "Yes that is correct." Later in life she gave me advice about work. I wanted to quit. She helped me hang in there.

I used to stop by her apartment in Covenant House, before going to work. She served me a big bowl of fruit every morning. I continued seeing her at the nursing home. She loved my visits. She said, "It gives me a lift." It took us a long time to say goodbye. Sometimes she called me Jeffanoo.

Philosophy of Teaching Bibliography

1) Wong, Harry K., and Rosemary T. Wong. *The First Days of School: How to Be an Effective Teacher*. Harry K. Wong Publications, 2009.

2) Zemelman, Steven, et al. *Best Practice: Bringing Standards to Life in America's Classrooms*. Heinemann, 2012.

3) Daniels, Harvey, and Marilyn Bizar. *Teaching the Best Practice Way: Methods That Matter, K-12*. Stenhouse Publishers, 2005.

4) Oakes, Jeannie, and Martin Lipton. *Teaching to Change the World*. McGraw-Hill Higher Education, 2007.

CPSIA information can be obtained
at www.ICGtesting.com
Printed in the USA
FSHW020516271020
75178FS